PONDS
AND
STREAMS

JOHN STIDWORTHY

Illustrated by
MICK LOATES and ALAN MALE

Troll Associates

Nature Club Notes

When you first view a pond or stream there may seem to be little wildlife other than the plants. Don't be fooled. A lot is there for you to discover. If you approach clumsily, animals may feel your vibrations. Any animal scurrying for cover is a warning to other animals, even if it is only thinking of its own safety! Be quiet and move slowly if you wish to spot wildlife.

Freshwater animals are often well-disguised and many are tiny. Therefore, they are hard to spot. Sharp eyes and ears are the best equipment a Nature Club member can take on a field trip. Knowledge of who lives where is also important, but this comes with experience. Be on the watch for telltale signs, like tracks in the mud, and develop the skills of a detective.

A small net with fine mesh is best for catching water animals. For the tiniest species you may need one with a tube on the end. The animals become trapped in the tube rather than being squashed in the mesh. But don't forget to search in the mud. A magnifying glass will help you to examine your smaller discoveries, and a reference book will help you identify what you find.

A glass jar full of fresh water can hold your catch while you examine it. A white tray underneath may make the animals easier to see. But do not let them get too warm, and put them back before too long.

Be careful where you walk. Water can be very dangerous, and the mud may be softer than you think.

Library of Congress Cataloging-in-Publication Data

Stidworthy, John, (date)
  Ponds & streams / by John Stidworthy; illustrated by Mick Loates
& Alan Male.
    p.   cm.—(The Nature club)
  Summary: Describes the characteristics of various animals that
live in or around ponds and streams.
  ISBN 0-8167-1963-2 (lib. bdg.)   ISBN 0-8167-1964-0 (pbk.)
  1. Pond ecology—Juvenile literature.   2. Stream ecology—Juvenile
literature. [1. Pond animals. 2. Stream animals.] I. Loates,
Mick, ill. II. Male, Alan, ill. III. Title. IV. Title: Ponds and
streams. V. Series.
QH541.5.P63S74   1990
574.5′26322—dc20   89-20331

Published by Troll Associates

Designed by Cooper Wilson, London
Design consultant James Marks

Printed in the U.S.A.

10 9 8 7 6 5 4 3

Contents

Nature Club Notes 2

Running Water 4

Quiet Waters 6

Exploring Ponds and Streams 8

Microscopic Water Life 10

Breathing in Water 12

At the Surface 14

In the Mud 16

Plant Eaters 18

Meat Eaters and Blood Suckers 20

Breeding 23

Young Animals 24

Making the Change 26

The Water's Edge 28

Glossary 30

Index 31

Running Water

The *source*, or beginning, of a stream is in the hills. The clear water trickling out of the ground is joined by other streams and soon a small torrent is gushing down the valley. As it swirls around the boulders its force carries smaller stones along with it.

Dipper

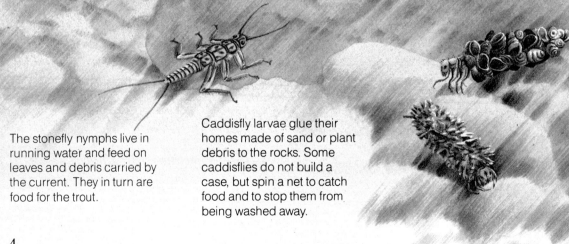

The stonefly nymphs live in running water and feed on leaves and debris carried by the current. They in turn are food for the trout.

Caddisfly larvae glue their homes made of sand or plant debris to the rocks. Some caddisflies do not build a case, but spin a net to catch food and to stop them from being washed away.

Few plants can root or grow in the tugging water, but willow moss may coat some boulders. A casual glance will detect no life, but closer examination will uncover animals who have learned to live with, or have *adapted* to, these conditions. Most of them are flat so they can shelter under stones from the strong current. Others have suction pads to hold them to the rocks. The streamlined shape of the trout enables it to battle against the flow.

This is home to the dipper, the only bird that can walk underwater. With its wings partly spread to hold it down, it searches the bottom for insects to eat.

Not many fish like strong-flowing streams, but the trout, with its torpedo-shaped body, can swim against the current.

If the flow is not too fast, little fish like the bullhead may make a home under the stones.

Quiet Waters

When the stream reaches a flatter area it slows. The stones and soil it has dragged along are dropped on the stream bed. Now the plants can fix their roots into the mud and send shoots to the surface. Without the strong current, it is easier for them to survive.

The web of life, or *ecology*, of a slow-moving stream is similar to that of a pond. Many of the same animals can live in both places. Each species is part of a community, competing with others for its food and other needs. Plants get their food from the mud and from sunlight. But when the water becomes too cold in winter, they stop growing. Plants provide homes and food for the animals, and the animals are food for each other. Smaller animals are usually dinner for larger ones.

Larger fish become food for anglers. Smaller ones may fall victim to the kingfisher as it patrols the riverbank. The heron also gets a better view of its prey in calmer waters. The food chain continues through a menu of newts, tadpoles, spiders, insects, and bugs.

Slow-moving or still water may be difficult for animals to live in because it has less oxygen for them to breathe. If it is warm or dirty, it holds even less. Almost nothing can survive in water badly polluted by sewage or chemicals.

Kingfisher

These waterweeds provide a jungle for a whole community of animals to live and feed.

Backswimmer

Exploring Ponds and Streams

Animals have many different alarm calls to warn others of the presence of an intruder. The alarm may only be meant for its mate or family, but it will alert the whole community. A beaver slapping its tail on water is as effective as an air-raid warning. You will need to be stealthy.

Fish have a larger field of vision than we do, so they may see you before you see them. Although they don't have ears like ours, fish have inner ears and can hear. *Camouflage*, which is the design Nature gives an animal to make it look like its surroundings, is often its best defense. You will not be able to spot the animal unless you look hard.

Around the water's edge, bulrushes and reeds provide shelter for birds' nests and all kinds of animals. The gallinule

The young chicks snuggle together under the grebe's wings.

8

has long toes to spread its weight on the marshy ground. Its larger relative, the coot, has big lobes on its toes to help it swim. The gallinule can only move quickly by jerking its head back and forth as it swims. Grebes carry their young on their backs. All these birds build platform nests, some floating on the water.

On sunny days a snake may be *basking* on the bank. Snakes like to catch fish and frogs. If you disturb one, it may dive into the water. Some animals only visit the water at dusk, but they may leave footprints for you to find.

Gallinule

Water Vole

Grass Snake

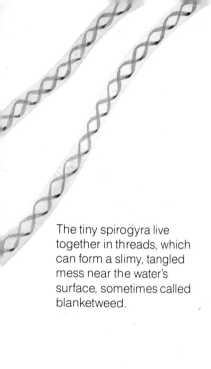

Microscopic Water Life

Pond water contains numerous plants and animals too small to be seen with the human eye. If you look at a drop of pond water through a *microscope*, you may see some. Tiny plants with no roots or leaves are called *algae*. They float in the water, or cover other plants, and use light near the surface to make food and grow. They, in turn, become food for small animals.

Euglena and volvox are algae known as *flagellates*. They move by beating tiny whiplike extensions, from which they get their name. Euglena has a mouth groove, but no one has seen it being used to catch food. Because it has both plant and animal features, some scientists believe euglena may be the link between the plant and animal worlds. Volvox live in

The tiny spirogyra live together in threads, which can form a slimy, tangled mess near the water's surface, sometimes called blanketweed.

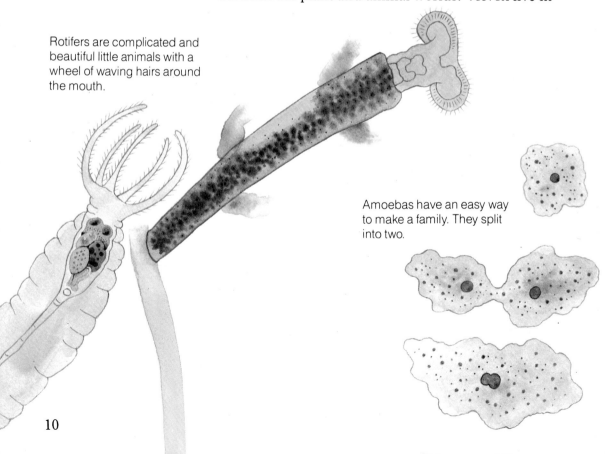

Rotifers are complicated and beautiful little animals with a wheel of waving hairs around the mouth.

Amoebas have an easy way to make a family. They split into two.

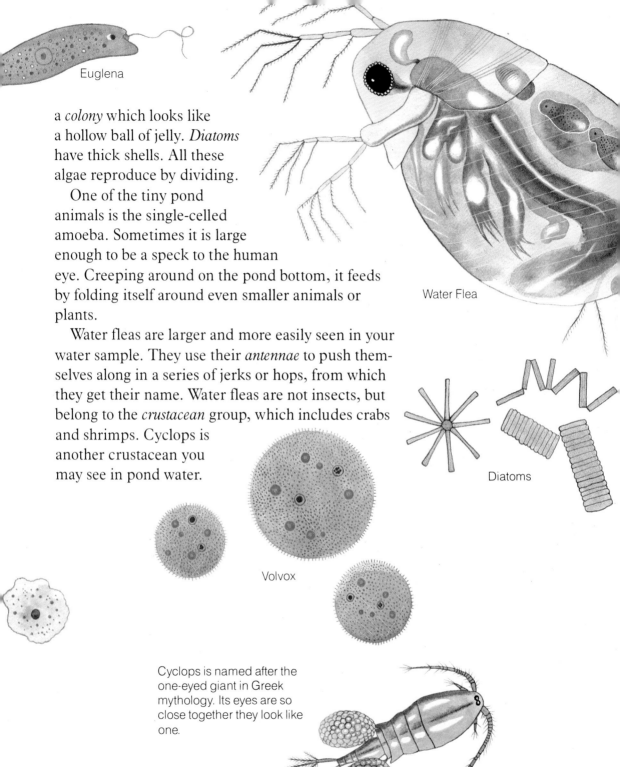

Euglena

a *colony* which looks like
a hollow ball of jelly. *Diatoms*
have thick shells. All these
algae reproduce by dividing.

One of the tiny pond
animals is the single-celled
amoeba. Sometimes it is large
enough to be a speck to the human
eye. Creeping around on the pond bottom, it feeds
by folding itself around even smaller animals or
plants.

Water fleas are larger and more easily seen in your
water sample. They use their *antennae* to push themselves along in a series of jerks or hops, from which
they get their name. Water fleas are not insects, but
belong to the *crustacean* group, which includes crabs
and shrimps. Cyclops is
another crustacean you
may see in pond water.

Water Flea

Diatoms

Volvox

Cyclops is named after the
one-eyed giant in Greek
mythology. Its eyes are so
close together they look like
one.

11

Breathing in Water

Tiny animals in water need no special organs to breathe. They are so small that the little oxygen they need can be absorbed through their skins. Larger water animals need special organs to get enough oxygen.

Fish gulp water through their mouths and pass it through *gills* in the sides of their body. The gills consist of many threads of folded skin supported by gristle. The folds provide the largest possible surface in a small area to absorb the oxygen from the water and pass it directly into the fish's blood. Water containing waste carbon dioxide exits from under the gill cover. Tadpoles and some insects in their *larva* stage also have gills, but of different shapes and in different places.

Diving Beetle

Mosquito larvae have breathing tubes on their tails. Since they float near the surface, the tubes are quite short.

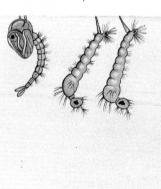

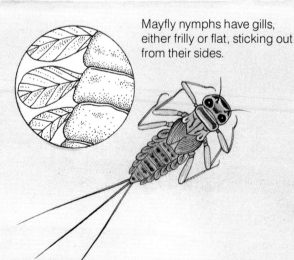

Mayfly nymphs have gills, either frilly or flat, sticking out from their sides.

Many water insects need more oxygen than water can provide, so they breathe air. Spiders diving beneath the surface trap air in their body hairs to take down with them. Freshwater beetles carry their air supply underwater in the form of an air bubble trapped under their wing covers. Without the buoyancy of their air bubble they are literally sunk. It keeps them light enough to swim back to the surface. Most insects renew their air supply regularly by sticking their rear end through the water surface. An exception is the silver diving beetle, which pokes its head out. By folding its antennae along grooves in its body it makes tubes for the air to pass to the wing cases. Mosquito larvae stick a little breathing tube above the surface, like a natural snorkel.

The Rat-tailed maggot is the larva of a fly. It can live in filthy water. At the end of its body is a long breathing tube which can reach right to the surface from the mud where it sits.

Silver Diving Beetle

Diving Beetle

At the Surface

If you see a lot of birds on the water's surface, you know there is plenty of food below. Swans and ducks upend, sticking their tails in the air as they search for underwater plants. Ducks eat some small water animals, too. Grebes dive underwater to catch their food. A closer look at birds' beaks will give you a clue as to what they eat. Are they sharp to grab fish? Or are they flat to scoop up algae? Many smaller animals live on the surface of ponds and in the still waters of streams. Pond skaters are so light that the water can support them. Their long, narrow legs have pads made of hair at the end. These trap air and hold the insect on top of the water. Like all insects, a pond skater has six legs, but you may only notice four. Its hind legs act as rudders and its middle pair as oars. The front legs are tucked under its head, ready to grab small insects unlucky enough to fall in the water.

Springtails

The pond skater is eating a mosquito larva.

14

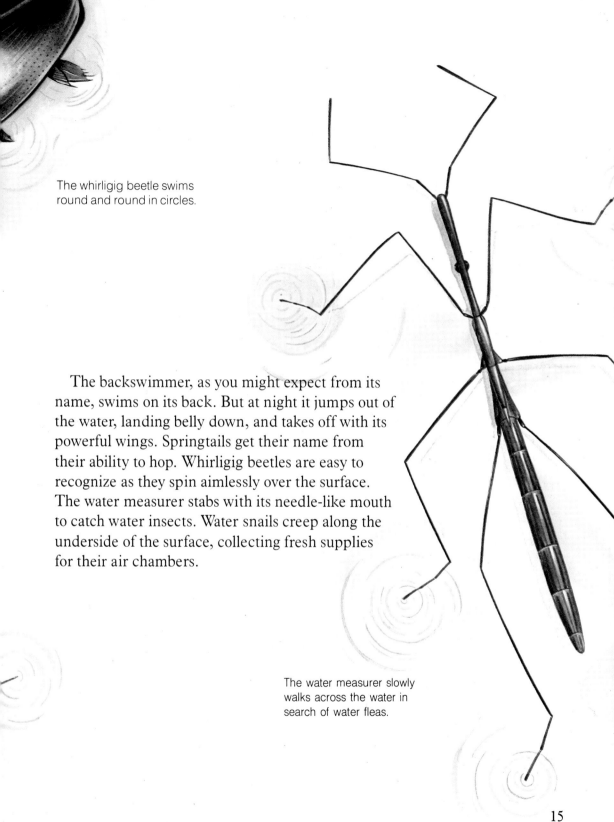

The whirligig beetle swims round and round in circles.

The backswimmer, as you might expect from its name, swims on its back. But at night it jumps out of the water, landing belly down, and takes off with its powerful wings. Springtails get their name from their ability to hop. Whirligig beetles are easy to recognize as they spin aimlessly over the surface. The water measurer stabs with its needle-like mouth to catch water insects. Water snails creep along the underside of the surface, collecting fresh supplies for their air chambers.

The water measurer slowly walks across the water in search of water fleas.

In the Mud

Even in winter, you may be surprised at how much life is contained in a scoop of mud from the bottom of a pond or river. *Hibernating* beetles take a rest from the cold there. Insect larvae nestle in the mud before continuing their development in the warmer months. You will also find roots and plant buds awaiting the spring.

In summer, you can find active insect larvae, perhaps of mayflies or dragonflies. Many kinds of worms burrow in the mud, feeding on the decaying matter that has fallen to the bottom of the water. Some look similar to earthworms, while others are tiny and colorless. Even scientists have difficulty recognizing them all. The tubifex sludge worm lives in thick mud. It is red because it has hemoglobin in its body. This is the red substance that carries the oxygen in your blood. Tubifex worms live in mud tubes with their tails sticking up into the water. They use these waving tails as gills.

Flatworms are meat eaters. Like tubifex worms they can reproduce by splitting in two.

You can find flatworms crawling over mud or on leaves. If you look down at its head, you may notice a pair of "horns" and a pair of simple eyes. They take in food through a mouth which lies well back on their belly.

Mud is also home to shellfish. The big freshwater mussels feed and breathe by sucking in water and passing it over large gills before sending it out again. Microscopic pieces of food are filtered out by the gills. Because mussels grow faster in summer than in winter, their shells have rings which can help you calculate their age.

The tubifex worm can live in polluted water where little else survives, and there you may find thousands squirming together in a tangled mass.

Mussels have two tubes which they push up into the water to feed. One is a water inlet, and the other an outlet.

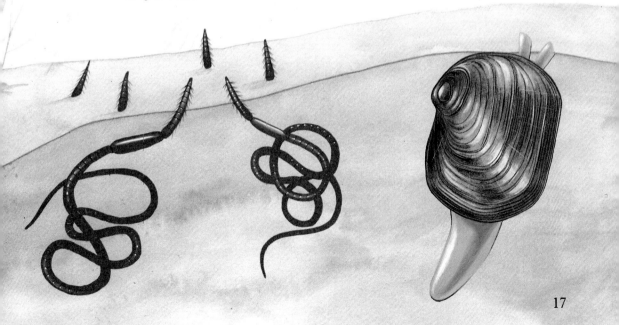

Plant Eaters

Several rodents live in and around water. Rodents are gnawing animals with four chisel-shaped front teeth. They all eat plant food. Just about anything goes – roots, bulbs, seeds, stalks, leaves, and even tree bark. Many also eat insects and small animals. Rodents' gnawing teeth grow throughout their lives, but seemingly endless munching grinds them to a constant length. Most rodents produce large families because so many fall victim to larger animals.

Perhaps the best known water rodent is the beaver. It is common in North America and found in parts of Europe. European beavers live in burrows, but their North American cousins build dams, often

Beavers have webbed feet for swimming and big flattened tails. The greasy fur is waterproof. They can close their noses when they dive.

Muskrat

creating large ponds behind them. These provide new homes for many other animals. The coypu was originally a South American species that has been introduced in many parts of the world for its fur, as have North American muskrats. Rats, voles, and mice also scurry around the water's edge.

Ducks and swans also live on plant food, and snails nibble away at the algae. Snails have long narrow tongues which are covered with tiny hard "teeth." The tongue is used like a file to rasp at the food. Some freshwater snails have gills, but ramshorn and pond snails breathe with a kind of lung. You may see them coming to the surface for fresh air. Snails lay numerous eggs in a blob of firm jelly on a leaf or stone. Sometimes you can see the baby snails developing.

Most of the water insects are meat eaters. An exception is the lesser water boatman, which is often found near the bottom feeding on algae and plant remains.

Snails' eggs in jelly are attached to the leaves.

Ramshorn Snail

Snails feed on weeds and on the algae growing on rocks.

Great Pond Snail

Diving Beetle
Larva

Meat Eaters and Blood Suckers

Insects are among the fiercest hunters. Hidden on the water's bottom, the dragonfly larva awaits its prey. It has a long, hinged lower jaw with two ferocious fangs at the end. If unsuspecting insects, tadpoles, or even fish come within reach, the jaw shoots out to grab them.

Another vicious insect is the diving beetle. The adults have powerful jaws, but the larvae are larger than the adults and possibly more dangerous. Their jaws are strong pincers which seize the prey and inject saliva into it. The saliva paralyzes the victim and starts to digest it, so its juices can be sucked out by the larva. Diving beetles and their larvae can overpower prey larger than themselves.

Many leeches feed on the blood of other animals, and even on human blood if they get a chance. The leech's smooth body has a sucker at each end. It moves by clamping its rear end to one surface and stretching its front sucker until it finds another. Then it brings up its rear end. The front sucker has teeth which sink into the victim to draw blood.

The dragonfly larva has caught a stickleback for its dinner.

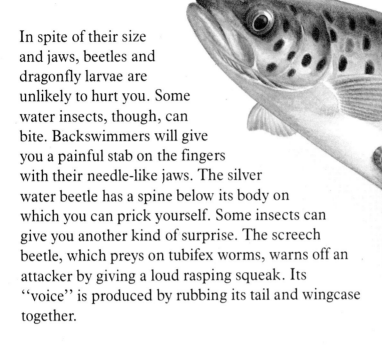

In spite of their size
and jaws, beetles and
dragonfly larvae are
unlikely to hurt you. Some
water insects, though, can
bite. Backswimmers will give
you a painful stab on the fingers
with their needle-like jaws. The silver
water beetle has a spine below its body on
which you can prick yourself. Some insects can
give you another kind of surprise. The screech
beetle, which preys on tubifex worms, warns off an
attacker by giving a loud rasping squeak. Its
"voice" is produced by rubbing its tail and wingcase
together.

Leeches are a type of worm.
This one is sucking blood
from a fish. Other kinds
swallow prey such as insect
larvae whole.

Backswimmer

Otter swimming underwater
in search of food.

Ponds and streams provide
rich pickings for larger animals
too. Otters and mink are two of the
large meat eaters. Both feed on fish, but
mink also like rodents and birds. Unless you
are lucky, you will not see these animals, as
they work night shifts. But you may spot the
remains of their food, or droppings or tracks.
One bird you may see is the tall heron as it stalks
fish in shallow water.

Stickleback

Breeding

In the spring many animals come to ponds to breed. Frogs and newts often return to the pond where they hatched. The male newt attracts a female by performing a wiggling dance which sends his scent toward her. Unlike the silent newts, frogs attract their mates with noise. Frog "songs" vary from simple croaks to the whistle of the North American peeper. The European common frog sounds like a small motorbike.

Animals that live in ponds all year round also mate in the spring. The male stickleback can be recognized by his red throat. After building a nest on the pond bottom, he attracts a female by dancing for her. Once she has laid eggs in his nest, he has no further use for her. He guards the nest fiercely, and should his young stray he gathers them in his mouth and spits them out close to the nest without hurting them.

Newt

Stickleback trying to attract a female.

23

Young Animals

Some of the young animals you discover in ponds and streams may take to the air as adults. Dragonflies, mayflies, and even some moths are just a few of the insects that have aquatic young. Tadpoles will leave the water as frogs or toads to continue their life on land. But the majority of wildlife in a pond or stream will stay there forever because they cannot survive out of water. Many even need the exact surroundings in which they were born.

Some of the shortest, fattest, and ugliest young animals become the most beautiful adults. When the young dragonfly hatches from an egg, it has the same features as the adult, but it is smaller and has no wings. It is called a *nymph*. Dragonfly nymphs are camouflaged by being brown or yellow-green. The end of the body is hollow to take in water. By forcing the water out again, dragonfly nymphs can

This aquatic moth caterpillar makes its home by gluing two pieces of leaf together.

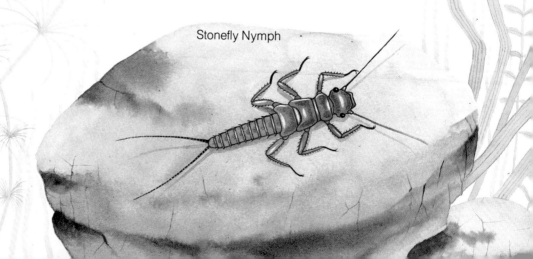

Stonefly Nymph

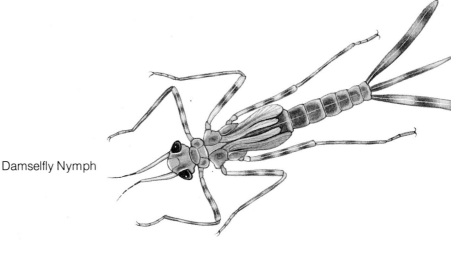

Damselfly Nymph

The caddisfly larva builds a home around itself.

propel themselves forward like jets. The more delicate damselfly nymph has to wiggle its body from side to side to swim. Both it and the mayfly nymph have three "tails" at the end of their bodies. These are really breathing organs. The stonefly nymph, which lives under stones in fast streams, has only two "tails."

Amphibians are animals that lead a double life. They are at home on land and in water. Frogs and newts are amphibians. You may have seen frogs' eggs in a mass of jelly attached to water plants. When hatched, the young start their lives in water as tadpoles breathing through gills, but as adults they develop legs and feet and breathe through lungs.

Caddisfly larva without its cover.

Making the Change

Dragonfly *nymphs* live in water for up to five years. As they grow they molt, or shed their skins, several times. If you search carefully among the water plants, you may discover some outgrown skins.

Before it changes into a full-grown dragonfly the nymph crawls out of the water and up a reed or stick. Here it rests and dries in the sun. Soon the skin splits, and out comes a new adult. At first it is soft and its wings are crumpled. It waits for its skin to harden and the wings to spread. Then, with a flash of wings, it is off. You may have to be up early in the morning to see the event. After two weeks, the dragonfly's full colors develop, but by summer's end it will be dead.

A swarm of delicate flying insects at the water's edge are likely to be mayflies. Mayflies are the only insects to go through two winged stages. The nymph becomes a *dun*, which looks like the adult but is covered with a dull skin.

It leaves the water and flies shakily to a plant or stone. There it molts again, and the shiny adult emerges, but it has only a few hours to live. The swarms perform courtship dances, after which the females let eggs drop on the water. Death follows shortly afterward.

While nymphs may live years for such a short adult life, frogs pass through all stages, from spawn to frog, in a few weeks. If they survive the many predators wishing to eat them they can live for 10 years. Some newts can live for 25 years.

Tadpoles grow legs and develop lungs. Slowly the tail disappears. Soon the tadpole is a small frog, ready to emerge on land.

Frogs' eggs

Tiny tadpoles hatch from frogs' eggs. They swim by wriggling their tails.

The Water's Edge

Now you know some of the plants and animals that live in and around water. Nature Club members who go out to look for them are certain to discover even more.

You may not be the only visitor to the water's edge. Because ponds and streams are so full of life, other animals go there to search for food. In summer, swallows and martins swoop low over the banks and scoop the water's surface in their constant search for insects. Wagtails are also expert insect catchers. You might see them hunting along the bank or jumping into the air to catch their prey. Seagulls often come to inland waters. They are not fussy about what they eat as long as the food is plentiful.

When nest building, swallows collect mud from the water's edge. Some of the many insects hovering above the water will become food for their young.

Raccoons feed mainly at night. They are good climbers and can swim if they need to.

Foxes eat anything available: rabbits, voles, birds and their eggs, insects, and fruit and berries as well.

Foxes may prowl the bank at night looking for birds and their eggs to provide an easy supper. In North America, and in a few parts of Europe where they have been introduced, raccoons can be found at the water's edge. They may look as if they are washing their hands, but actually their sensitive fingers are feeling for small prey such as crayfish and frogs.

Other animals visit water just to drink. During the day, flocks of birds may come, and in the evening, deer may arrive. Even while they drink, their noses and ears nervously test the surroundings for danger. They never know what creature might visit the water's edge next.

Deer come down to the water's edge for an evening drink.

Yellow Wagtail

All wagtails can be recognized by their tails, which bob up and down as they dart about in search of food.

Glossary

adapt   the way an animal changes its behavior, or even its body, to suit its living conditions.

algae   tiny plants without roots or leaves. Some float in the water, others may be attached to stones or weeds. Many are single-celled, some live in colonies.

amphibian   an animal which is at home both in water and on land.

antennae   the long feelers that crustaceans or insects have on their heads.

basking   lying in the sun to warm up the body.

camouflage   an animal's disguise which hides it from its enemies.

colonies   groups of animals or plants that live together as a unit but remain separate individuals.

crustacean   the group of animals that includes crabs, lobsters and shrimps. They have a hard skin and jointed legs. Most crustaceans live in the sea or in fresh water.

diatoms   single-celled algae which have a tiny two-part shell like the base and lid of a pillbox. Some live singly, others in colonies.

dun   the immature adult of a mayfly.

ecology   the way in which plants and animals co-exist.

flagellate   a microscopic animal which beats its whiplike extensions to move through the water.

gills   organs which water animals use for obtaining oxygen to breathe. Basically they are areas of thin skin where oxygen can easily get into the body. They may be different shapes or in different places in different groups of animals.

hibernation   a sleeplike state during the winter, in which the workings of the body slow down.

larva   a stage in the life of many animals after they hatch from the egg, and before they develop the adult type of body. If there are more than one, they are called **larvae.** In insects, larvae are young that make a sudden change to the pupa, and adult stages, rather than changing gradually as a nymph does.

microscope   an instrument with a combination of lenses which allows you to see a greatly magnified image of an object placed under it. With it you can see many details invisible to the naked eye.

molt   to shed an outside skin which has become too small.

nymph   a young insect of a type that goes through a series of molts as it grows, making a gradual change to adult appearance. Dragonflies, mayflies and grasshoppers have this type of young.

pupa   a resting stage in the development of some insects, such as flies and butterflies, between the larva and the adult stages. If there is more than one, they are called pupae.

Index

algae, *10, 19, 30*
amoeba, *10, 11*
backswimmer, *7, 15, 21*
beaver, *8, 18*
beetle,
    diving, *12, 13, 20*
    larva, *20*
    screech, *21*
    silver, *13, 21*
    whirligig, *14, 15*
bullhead, *5*
bulrush, *8*
caddisfly, larva *4, 25*
coot, *9*
coypu, *19*
crab, *11*
crayfish, *29*
crustacean, *11, 30*
cyclops, *11*
deer, *29*
diatom, *11, 30*
dipper, *4, 5*
dragonfly, *16, 24, 25, 26*
    larva or nymph, *16*
    20, 21, 24, 25, 26
duck, *14, 19*
dun, *26, 30*
euglena, *10, 11*
fish,
    bullhead, *5*
    trout, *5*
flagellate, *10, 30*
flatworm, *16, 17*
fox, *28, 29*

frog, *9, 23, 25, 27, 29*
    common, *23*
    eggs, *27*
    peeper, *23*
gallinule, *8, 9*
grebe, *8, 9, 14*
heron, *7, 22*
kingfisher, *7*
leech, *20, 21*
martin, *28*
mayfly, *16, 24, 26*
    dun, *26*
    larva or nymph, *12, 16*
    25, 26, 27
midge, *4*
mink, *22*
mosquito,
    larva, *12, 13*
moth, caterpillar, *24*
mouse, *19*
muskrat, *18, 19*
mussel, *17*
newt, *7, 23, 25, 27*
nymph, *24, 26, 27, 30*
    damselfly, *25*
    dragonfly, *24, 26*
    mayfly, *12, 25*
    stonefly, *7, 24, 25*
otter, *22*
pond skater, *14*
raccoon, *28, 29*
rat, *19*
rat-tailed maggot, *13*
rotifers, *10*

screech beetle, *21*
shrimp, *11*
snail, *15*
    great pond, *19*
    ramshorn, *19*
    water, *15*
snake,
    grass, *9*
spawn, *27*
spider, *7, 13*
spirogyra, *10*
springtail, *14, 15*
stickleback, *20, 22, 23*
stonefly, nymph, *7, 24, 25*
swallow, *28*
swan, *14, 19*
tadpole, *7, 12, 20, 24, 25, 27*
toad, *24*
trout, *5*
tubifex worm, *16, 17, 21*
vole, *19, 28*
    water, *9*
volvox, *10, 11*
wagtail, *28, 29*
    yellow, *29*
water boatman, lesser, *19*
water flea, *11*
water strider, *15*
whirligig beetle, *14, 15*
worm, *16*
    earth, *16*
    flat, *16, 17*
    tubifex, *16, 17, 21*